Hoover Tig

Male Tiger
Born 4/23/2004 - Rescued 4/23/2016
Crossed the Rainbow Bridge 10/07/2019

What's It Worth to You?

Imagine opening your eyes for the very first time. As you struggle to understand what is going on, you hear an all too familiar voice crying out for you. In your rear view, you see your mother crying out, confused, desperately trying to reach out for you. Suddenly, you realize that there are unfamiliar arms wrapped around you; a cold, rough, heartless grip on you as you wonder what will happen next.

A steel cage with cold bars surrounding you from every side. Like minded terrified cubs who have been ripped from the love and comfort of their mothers. Starving and not knowing where your next meal is coming from or when for that matter. Being kicked, hit, whipped, and frightened into submission. Exhausted and barely given a moment to rest as you are made to perform for what feels like an eternity day in and day out. Crowds of people yelling, screaming, and cheering you on without a care in the world for your safety or wellbeing.

Could you imagine what it would be like to live this way for 11 years? Watching all of your friends suffer alongside you and knowing that there is nothing you can do. Over time, the only comfort you had, those other cubs raised in this horrible setting, dying, one by one, until you are the last one left. Alone with nowhere to go and nobody to turn to?

Hoover endured things in life that we as humans could never have overcome with the strength and dignity that he did. Yet, so many people know and see these horrors and just sit back and wait on the rest of the world to step in and make a difference. His strength was and will remain inspirational to so many around the world, and his fight made a difference with every single day he shared with us. So many souls were touched, and lives brightened by one magnificent tiger who was fortunate enough to make it out of the circus alive… something his companions were never given the chance to do.

As children, we are taught to admire these animals for how they have been presented to us. Big scary wild animals who are so "easily tamed" and trained to do fun tricks and daring stunts. We are taught that these animals are loved, adored, and all too eager to please people because they "want" to. We see them dressed up in ridiculous costume and we take them for rides, and all it cost us is a few dollars and a little bit of time. No big deal. Right?

The cost of that ride, that show, those couple of hours of your time has an unimaginable impact on these animals. You can always make back the few dollars you spent, but Hoover can never get those 11 years of abuse, neglect, starvation, and fear back. He cannot undo the scars from the beatings he endured. He cannot undo the muscle and bone damage or the stunt in growth that he had forced upon him, while living life out in a transport cage, and he cannot undo the damage from the multiple parasitic infections and lifelong intestinal damage he suffered either.

He did, however, have the opportunity to finally feel grass beneath his feet. He was able to swim in a cool spring fed lake and enjoy being catered to with great meals each and every day. He was able to finally know love and respect and be accepted for every part of who he was. He also became one of the world's biggest ambassadors against circus cruelty, and that all began in the year 2014, when things started to change and there was hope for Hoover for the very first time.

My question to you is what's the damage to these animals worth in your eyes?! Is the suffering this amazing Tiger, and so many other animals, had to endure really worth those few hours of "joy" and "pleasure" you had? Or will you be one of many who changes their mind and hears Hoovers story loud and clear. Someone who feels this deep within their soul and is willing to speak up on his behalf?

United, we can make a world of difference. The sad truth is that so many of us are caught up in our own minds, our own lives, our own dreams, and we convince ourselves that somewhere out there, enough people already care enough to make a difference. So, what's one voice? And that is why the world, our world, these animals' worlds and lives, are suffering to such a severe degree.

Your voice matters! Your heart, your thoughts, your efforts can make waves around the world. They can put an end to the cruelty that these precious souls suffer at the hand of human greed. They can save an entire species and they can set a new example for generations to come.

I for one, plan to see that difference through. To see hearts change and love and respect grow for these beautiful creatures and watch their species thrive in the wild, free of cages and free of the human hand, and I will do that in part, because Hoover deserves to have his memory honored in a beautiful way. What better way could you think of than to set his species free?!

Rest Peacefully Hoover. Your story will never cease to be told, and your spirit will continue to shine brightly.

~ HLKopacz ~

We do not know Hoover's exact story prior to his rescue but the above is rather typical of a circus tigers life story. The facts we do know are posted below.

OPERATION SPIRIT FREEDOM

In 2014, Animal Defenders International (ADI) had been on track to remove Hoover, who was originally named Juver (which translates to Hoover in English), and one other tiger from the Peruvian circus in a nationwide law enforcement operation. The circus caught wind of the hunt for them and went underground, making it very difficult to locate them. Hoover's journey to freedom finally began after months of searching, when a helpful citizen tipped off ADI with the location of the illegal circus act.

In April of 2015, a dramatic rescue ensued. Animal Defenders International and the Peruvian Wildlife Officials were finally able to seize Hoover. Sadly, Hoover was the sole survivor of an estimated six to twelve tigers in possession of Circo African in Peru. ADI contacted Big Cat Rescue and asked if we would like to become Hoover's forever home, and of course we said yes!

The process of importing a tiger into the United States took longer than we expected. A whole year went by, but we finally received the green light from the USFWS. During this time, Hoover had spent years locked up in deplorable conditions. He had never even felt grass beneath his feet. He had arrived at ADI's rescue center terrified, sick, and emaciated. He was full of parasites and had some severe parasite infections. After months of intensive veterinary care, rehabilitation, and exercise, Hoover has recovered well and is ready for the next step in his life. He had gained 50 lbs. over the year he resided with ADI.

Big Cat Rescue was thrilled to welcome Hoover to his new forever home. Arrangements were made and Hoover was set to fly into Miami from Lima and trucked across the state on April 23rd, 2016 which just happened to be his 12th birthday! Hoover arrived on an Avianca cargo plane that was full of Mother's Day flowers. As the plane entered landing space, Hoover was honored and welcomed by a 78-foot banner that stretched clear across the entrance to the Miami International Airport and welcomed him to Florida! The airport even arranged to have the local elementary school children to write letters and draw pictures to welcome him to his new home! He was escorted personally by the ADI's President/Co-Founder, Jan Creamer and her husband, ADI's Vice President, Tim Philips.

Following protocol and finally being clear to take Hoover home, Gale Ingham, Jamie Veronica, Marie Schoubert, and Afton Tasler were ready to get Hoover safely loaded up and strapped in for the ride back to Tampa. They kept a close eye on him all the way to Big Cat Rescue. He traveled well and never needed any type of sedation to keep him calm, although he was exhausted from the 24-hour trip.

Upon arrival to Big Cat Rescue, Hoover was welcomed by anxiously awaiting Staff, Volunteers, Keepers, and Press who were eager to see his story through. During preparation of his enclosure, they had decorated in celebration of his arrival and for his birthday. He even received an all-meat birthday cake! There were smiles everywhere as the truck pulled into the sanctuary. It took several people to help pull him off the truck as his weight (353 lbs.) and the cage he was in totaled 1000 lbs.!

Cameras were focused and all eyes were on Hoover as the door was lifted and he stepped foot into his spacious lakeside enclosure. He wasted no time in exploring the foliage and heavy greenery within the trees. This was likely the first time he has experienced any type of freedom and he had more than earned it. TJ tiger was quite curious of his new neighbor and could be seen peeking his head around to watch. Hoover made his way down to the lake after taking in the sights. Although he was a little unsure of going in, he thoroughly enjoyed a cold fresh drink followed up by a well-deserved nap!

Hoover had a heartbreaking life with an incredible story to share with the entire world, and that is exactly what happened. These are just a few quotes from some of the articles surrounding Hoover's rescue and arrival to Big Cat Rescue.

National Geographic wrote a story titled "Abused Circus Tiger Gets Fairy-Tale Ending" and continued on to highlight the tragedy of what he had endured living the life of a circus tiger, but how he came out on top of it all.

USA Today wrote a story titled "Rescued Circus Tiger Will Get Roaring Welcome at Miami Airport" and continued on to discuss the excitement and celebration of Hoover's arrival to the United States. They also highlighted the growing list of countries who were banning the use of wild animals in circuses.

Fox 13 News coverage was aired on the evening news broadcast, and they reported with the title "Tiger Rescued from Peruvian Circus Comes to Tampa" and announced that Big Cat Rescue would be welcoming their newest male tiger to the sanctuary! They went on to quote ADI's Jan Creamer in saying, "Hoover's story is one of the saddest stories of the whole rescue because originally that circus had 12 tigers and he is the only survivor."

Bay News 9 released an article that told of the remarkable dedication of ADI and their having not given up the hunt. ADI's Jan Creamer was quoted saying, "It turned into something of a riot, with the circus fighting back. The siege lasted about 8 or 9 hours, but we did eventually get him away." Bay News 9 went on to say that although the battle to get Hoover from the circus was over, the battle to save his life was not.

South Florida Reporter wrote an article titled "Rescued from Peruvian Circus, Hoover Tiger is Being Moved to Florida" and stated that after a lifetime full of suffering in a Peruvian circus, Hoover the tiger will finally be free. Hoover will get the best birthday present of all: a new start in life and a new home in America. ADI's Jan Creamer was quoted saying, "Hoover is the tiger that almost got away from us. The Peruvian circus went underground, so it was very difficult to track him down and rescue him from his sad life of pain and suffering. It is a privilege to bring Hoover, who turns 12 on Saturday, to Big Cat Rescue to begin his new chapter of his life happy and safe at this wonderful sanctuary. He has special needs and deserves special attention — and that is exactly the kind of care Big Cat Rescue does so well."

Mother Nature Networks article titled "Abused circus tiger gets happy home" highlights Operation Spirit Freedom and the journey of Hoover to the United States. Big Cat Rescues founder, Carole Baskin, was quoted saying "We are so happy to welcome Hoover and provide him with a safe, peaceful home at our sanctuary in Tampa. He will now spend the rest of his life enjoying the warm breezes of Florida, relaxing in the shady grass, lounging on his platforms, and cooling off in our lake. He will literally be a world away from the abuse he suffered most of his life."

Along with the above articles listed, there were many other reporters and types of media that covered Hoovers journey through Operation Spirit Freedom. He was and still remains a worldwide inspirational icon to many and provides us with the strength to continue to push for the Big Cat Public Safety Act to be passed.

December 2, 2016

Hoover Tiger had been noted to have his penis stuck out of the sheath. Dr. Justin Boorstein came in and sedated him to try and figure out what the problem was. This can be a serious problem to animals as it can dry up and even dying in some cases. The decision was made to go ahead and neuter him at the same time just in case there could be any relation to the current issue.

The next step was to put the penis back in the sheath. With this comes the risk of it popping back out so Dr. Boorstein placed a special kind of suture there that decreased the size of the hole. The suture will dissolve, and the hope is that whatever caused it to get stuck out in the first place, will have resolved itself by then.

He was placed on antibiotics and pain medications to get him through the healing phase comfortably and clear of any risk of infection.

An abdominal ultrasound was also done due to a history of loose stools and although all of them have tested negative for issue regarding it, this was a good time to go ahead and see if there was an obvious cause to the loose stools. Hoover did have some gastrointestinal issues that he arrived with so he may have just had loose stool as a side effect to that.

January 12, 2017

Hoover had complications following his first surgery for his penis, so Dr. Justin Boorstein came in and sedated him again for a condition called Paraphimosis. This condition is the inability to retract an extruded penis back into the preputial sheath. It had only been a few weeks since his first procedure, and now that the sutures had dissolved, the issue had occurred again. This meant finding a way to keep the penis inside the sheath.

Dr. Boorstein performed a procedure that meant sewing the side of his penis to the side of the prepuce (the protective sheath) which meant that his penis could not come out of the sheath. We were hoping that this would resolve the issue for right now at least.

Unfortunately, 2-3 weeks later, the problem reoccurred. We called upon the boarded surgeon, Dr. Hay, who had performed Mickey cougar's knee surgeries, and asked him for help with Hoover.

Hoover was sedated again and underwent surgery for a third time. Permanent sutures were sewn in multiple spots in Hoover's penis to lift the penis into the appropriate position and keep it there. The sheath was then sewn around the penis tightly enough to only allow the tip to be exposed so that he could properly urinate.

After Hoover woke up, he was taken back outside to his enclosure to recover. We were hopeful that this would permanently resolve the issue for him.

Hoover was a magnificent tiger who taught us all so much about strength, fight, love, and forgiveness. Upon his arrival to Big Cat Rescue, thousands of people from around the world tuned in to see him take his first steps into freedom. Watching the expressions on his face as he walked out of the transport and looked around brought tears of Joy to us all. Seeing him lean down and take his first few sips of cold fresh water from the spring fed lake and take his first swim was an unexplainable feeling. It was clear from the start that Hoover had already began changing lives, hearts, and opening eyes.

In March of 2019, Hoover developed a limp and began favoring his front left paw. The belief was that he had an ingrown dewclaw. All of his nails were trimmed down, but his dewclaw was in really rough shape. We learned that Hoover had not been shedding the sheaths on his claws in quite some time and that meant he would have to endure an extensive procedure.

At the same time, Dr. Boorstein noticed that Hoover had a red spot on his tongue. Airing on the side of caution, the spot was removed and sent out for testing. The results came back positive for a squamous cell carcinoma which is an aggressive cancer.

All margins had been hit, and everyone was hopeful that it would not return. Hoover made it through the procedure with ease and had to spend 10 days in the hospital recovery enclosure to keep his paws out of the dirt and water, along with a full course of antibiotics.

Although we hoped that this would take care of Hoover's limp, it unfortunately returned. On April 22, 2019, Dr. Boorstein sedated Hoover again to check on his dewclaw and decided it would require surgery this time. There was a small pocket of infection present and it was feared that his nail itself was dead, which was the case, along with the surrounding tissue. Hoover had to have his dewclaw amputated in hopes of preventing any further spread of infection. Following the amputation and debriding of the tissue, Hoover was placed on another round of antibiotics and a tissue sample was sent out for testing to be sure he did not have cancer.

Sadly, the results came back and the results showed that he did indeed have cancer. As if that was not bad enough, he had a squamous cell carcinoma which is incredibly aggressive and spreads quickly and deeply within the tissue. All margins were believed to be met and it was time for Hoover to focus on healing.

Poor Hoover had endured so much already in the short amount of time since his arrival, and our hearts broke as we realized that he was living on borrowed time. This became increasingly clear to us in August when Hoover suffered a setback and the cancer returned to the very same paw with a vengeance. After a difficult three-hour procedure, Hoover lost another toe on his foot in order to have enough healthy flesh to close the wound left following the debriding. Although the surgery went well, the prognosis was not good and all we could do was hope for the best. Hoover was 15 years old and it was determined that there was nothing much left to be done should the cancer return. He did not tolerate anesthesia well and would not be able to endure chemo or radiation.
After an extended stay in the recovery hospital, Hoover healed up and returned to his enclosure in September where he was adored and watched closely by all who loved him so much. His keepers and caretakers made sure that he was catered too, including meals in bed.

October 7, 2019

Hoover had developed a limp over the last week, so Dr. Justin came out to try and get him up and walking to see what could be done for him, if anything at all. There was enough concern, that Dr. Justin decided to go ahead and sedate him to look at his paw (that he has had cancer removed from twice) and do some x-rays to see what could have been causing the limp. Sadly, it did not take long to see that he not only had another mass on that foot, but the x-rays indicated that he had developed bone cancer as well.

Hoover Tiger had a really tough go over the last year, and the majority of his life in general. We are so glad that we were able to give him a couple of good years here at Big Cat Rescue where he could enjoy swimming in the lake, relaxing in the sun, and sleeping in the warm green grass. He has brought so much joy into all of our lives and proven a strong ambassador for the fight against the circus life and the inherited abuse that comes along with it.

At 15 years of age, and with cancer wearing away at his body, letting go was the most humane choice that could be made on his behalf. There was nothing else that could be done to provide him with comfort or quality and Hoover had let us know that it was his time. Through tears and a heavy heart, Dr. Justin euthanized our precious Peruvian Tiger, Hoover.

Big Cat Rescue Says Goodbye to Hoover our Beloved Peruvian Circus Tiger

We are beyond heartbroken to let everyone know that Dr. Justin has humanely euthanized our beloved 15-year-old tiger Hoover this morning.

Hoover suffered from several bouts of cancer in the last year or so and recently had to have toes removed on his front leg due to aggressive squamous cell carcinoma. Dr. Justin sedated Hoover this morning as he had just developed a limp and to check on how his paw was doing.

His necropsy showed the tumors in his paw had returned, and more had developed in just the past few weeks. His bones looked to cancer ridden as well. Tissues will be sent to the labs, but there is no doubt that cancer was ravaging our precious Hoover, and nothing was going to reverse that downhill spiral.

Here is Carole's note this morning:
At the risk of sounding crazy: Dragonflies Come for Hoover

Yesterday after working on reinstalling the Nest cam in the Windsong Memorial Hospital, I hopped on my bike to head back to the office. Just outside the hospital I was surrounded by about a dozen HUGE dragonflies. They looked like those military helicopters and they were all in a cluster, of about a six-foot circle, around my head. I stopped to say, "Hello" to them. I basked in their company for a moment and then as reality sank in, I asked, "Who are you here for?" No reply.

I waited a while until they circled off above the Windsong Memorial Hospital. I tried to recall who was on the list to see Dr. Justin Boorstein today. Loki the Savannah Cat needed to have some mats groomed off him. I wasn't sure if these dragonflies were old friends visiting or something more prophetic.
Hoover Tiger's nest cam has been down and so we haven't been able to see if his limping was better or worse since last week. The vet team decided to get Hoover up on his feet this morning to let Dr. Justin get a better look at him. Hoover had squamous cell carcinoma removed twice from one front leg (taking two of his toes) and now seemed to be limping on his good leg. The situation was bad enough that Dr. Justin wanted to get X-rays again and a better look at the surgery site.

What we found looks to be bone cancer in Hoover's back leg, and severe arthritis throughout all of his joints. He's on so much pain medication, we can't put him on anymore. This is no life for this majestic tiger and the decision was made to let him go.

Now I wonder if the dragonflies who came were the dozen or so tigers who were in the circus act with Hoover, when the owners took them on the run to keep them from being taken to sanctuaries. All but Hoover had died; eleven in all, before help arrived for Hoover. I feel deep sadness of this loss because he was such a great cat and so many loved him, but I think he's back with his clan and they are all pain free and worry free now. Rest in peace, Hoover.

Susan Bass - Director of Public Relations

PREVENTION

We know from 27 years of experience that we cannot rescue every big cat that needs a home, but together we can make a difference. The most effective way to put an end to the suffering of big cats in America and around the world is to give these cats a voice. YOU are their voice. We must pass the Big Cat Public

Safety Act banning the breeding of these precious lives in captivity. A cat born in captivity can never be released into the wild. They are doomed to live their lives out in cages, often in some of the most deplorable conditions you can imagine. These magnificent cats deserve better than that.

Make the Call of the Wild in honor of all the cats like Hoover. Let their story be your moral compass that guides you to fight to end the abuse these big cats face each and every day. Go to www.BigCatAct.com or text CATS to 52886 and speak up!

PHOTOS

Hoover flies into Miami International Airport (MIA) this evening and will arrive to a hero's welcome! Join Big Cat Rescue in thanking everyone at MIA for welcoming Hoover with this 78-foot sign over the entrance to the airport!!

Hoover at the ADI Rescue Center in Peru

Photos by Brittany Mira

Photos by Jamie Veronica

Photos by Mary Lou Geis

What a beautiful day for sun bathing!

Hmmm... Who is that I see going on vacation?

Meredith – Look at the size of that precious Hoover Paw

Photographer Unknown

TRIBUTES
These are some of the tributes posted on Hoover's bio page at
https://BigCatRescue.org/hoover/

Paula Drechsler - Am so sad to hear of Hoover passing! I am also so happy he got to spend his last years at BCR being loved (or shall I say adored) and cared for by all the angels at the sanctuary. He got to swim, feel grass on his feet, do what he wanted when he wanted. I am now imagining him running completely free of pain and suffering with no cage confining him. I feel compelled to make an extra Call of the Wild this week in his honor.

Edith Eckert - We all loved you, Hoover- especially your stubbornness, the way you had all the keepers wrapped around your paw, your total enjoyment of your Royal status, singing and swimming in the rain and of course, your curly tail! I'm glad the dragonflies were here to take you back home. RIP sweet, sweet boy. You left a huge paw print on my heart and a very precious memory of you kindly coming down from your platform to "chuff" at me on my first private tour. Thank you for that.

Joann Dolce - Hoover my beautiful boy, I love you so much and always will. You were forcefully disciplined and forced to do things until you had absolutely no spirit left in you. All at BCR took brilliant care of you and the rest of the world loved you til the end and always. No more living in this sick body. You are now new and free.

Michele Clay - Run free and wild to all your friends who are waiting for you. It was time for you to be a wild tiger again. We miss you Governor but now you job is to watch over us as we watched over you. ❤ ▨ say hi to everyone.

Angie Reese - Once again my heart is sadden and hurting. I am going to miss you beautiful big guy, Words cannot express how I feel right now but for my love I am going to try. I am going to miss your goofy antics and everything about you, You were and still are very much loved and will be missed. Rest In Peace beautiful boy. I know you will be happy and pain free now, Run with the wind Hoover, Say hello to all of our other big cats when you get to the bridge. You are very much loved and you will never be forgotten in our hearts and our minds. My heart and love goes out to everyone at BCR, Love you all for all you do for these magnificent beings. RIP Hoover. I love you.

Ruthanne Case Suttlehan - Hoover, The Governor, that tail of yours! Will miss you so.

Linda Greene - God Bless Your Sweet Heart Precious Hoover ... You will be So Missed. Have Fun in Heaven Buddy with all your Fellow Cats. We are so Thankful for the time we had with you. We are also so Thankful for Everyone at BCR, Carole, The Staff, Keepers, Volunteers, Interns, Vets ...Thank God all of these Precious Animals have been Blessed with All the Love & Care you all have shown and continue to show to all these Majestic Animals!

Lori Anderson - We all loved you so much Hoover! You will forever be missed. Such a beautiful soul...such a tragic life. I'm so happy that you were able to find a peaceful place to call home for your last few years of life at BCR. From the moment you arrived until your last breath you were surrounded by love. Run free Hoovie - something you couldn't do on earth. RIP :' (

Carol Carlisle - Hoovie.... There is nothing I can say that will lessen the loss I feel. You will always be in my heart, my love goes with you to your new home. Thank You for being part of my life for a time for sharing your beauty and spirit. People would say you are just an animal but oh you are so much more, you and your kind were a gift from God and it shone from your eyes and in your exquisite form. Our world is emptier every time we lose one of you. You have gone home Hoovie, but I hope to see you again. Love and kisses sent on desert winds, forever.

Emma Betts - So sad to hear that the lovely Hoovie doo is no longer with us. I had such a soft spot for the governor, he brought me to Big Cat Rescue. His story so touching as he appeared so content once he had a taste of life outside his (circus prison) his first paw dip in the water, his love of breakfast in bed, the gentle way he ate his food, his stubbornness at times. RIP Hoover, always remembered, never forgotten. Sweet dreams.

Dk Foster - Your story inspired many and educated others. I wish we had more time with you dear Hoovie. Run free and happy sweet Governor. You will be missed but not forgotten

Amber Peterson - Very sad that Hoover is gone. He was the first Big Cat we saw at BCR. so majestic and such a wonderful tiger. very, very sad.

Debbie Kaz - Such a beautiful soul that brought us such joy. Thank you all for making his last years his best year!

Colleen Morris - Run free beautiful boy!!! You are now at peace! Next to Joseph you were my favorite and will be so missed!!!

Cathy Cotton - Hoover felt like family - I even got to know his markings. Will miss you baby. So sad...

Jessica Marks - Hoover was the first of your tigers I ever drew, not knowing then that in less than two years he would go from one of 6 tigers boys to the only male tiger on property. And now he follows the many tiger boys I got to know and love in the two years I've followed BCR: Andy, Andre, Arthur, Seth, and the dear gentle Zeus.

I used to grin seeing Hoover swipe at the feeding sticks as he lived at tiger lake, wearing a new path into the grass showing how much he would stay just out of the reach of keepers trying to feed him. But then I saw the footage of his circus performances where a stick was used to cruelly force him to do tricks, and suddenly I understood why he reacted as he did to those feeding sticks, even if it was now with calm playfulness.

Our dear governor will be forever missed, but I'm glad he's no longer in pain.
Run free, dear Hoover, no more sticks will ever come to your face, no more bars will ever come between you and freedom, no more crowds will ogle you, and no one will ever pay to see you perform ever again, and be at peace.

Viewer Bonnie - One chilly morning back in December of 2018, I was scrolling through my newsfeed on Facebook and a post/video caught my eye, regarding a tiger rescue. The tiger's name was Hoover and he was being rescued from a circus in Peru. From that day on, I fell in love with a tiger named Hoover. From viewing that post/video, I was fortunate enough to discover Big Cat Rescue. Hoover was special to me in so many ways.

He not only touched my heart, he touched my soul. My daily routine would consist of viewing his web cam, reading posts, or watching videos where he was the featured cat. All was right in the world, as long as my Hoover was safe, loved, and cared for. Hoover will remain in my heart forever and I miss him so much!

Everywhere I go, Hoover is right there with me, reminding me to be strong, courageous, and never give up on myself no matter what odds come against me. RIP precious Hoover. You truly were a one of a kind tiger.

Keeper Coordinator Lynda Licht - 10:45am Sunday 10/6/19

Me: Hello Hoover my love. Would you like to finish eating your breakfast now?

Hoover (grumbling and stretching as he rolls over to sit up): If I have to.. (After several minutes and passing meat on a long stick to him...)

Me: Last drummie. Come on, you need your calcium.

Hoover: CRUNCH. Gulp.

Me: You are so good. Can you come out and take a walk with me? I need to make a video so the vets can see how you are doing.

Hoover: (yawning, stretching...making a motion like he might get up...but flops back over on his side) No, I just wanna lay here. My paw is bothering me (licks it some) and my legs hurt.

Me: You know I love you very much, right?

Hoover (looks right at me): uh-huh.

Me: They are going to come look at you tomorrow. You need to be brave.

Hoover: Haven't I always been?

Me: Yes, my love. You are the bravest boy ever. Hey (changing the subject) remember when you were at tiger lake and you wouldn't come over to eat right away and the camera caught me practicing my samba routine? Your fans got a kick out of that!

Hoover: sigh...

Me: Remember when you lived on tiger row and you loved laying on that tall platform but you'd always come down for me and eat in lockout like a big boy tiger?

Hoover: rrrrrr....I wanted to please you

Me: Remember all those Friday nights I'd come to feed you and it'd be getting late and dark and you'd finally come over and sit by the edge of the enclosure with me?
Hoover: I'm getting sleepy....can't I go back to my nap now?

Me: Sure thing handsome. Sleep well

I'd come back later at 12:30 and again at 3:30. Hoover was still snoozing. I didn't have the heart to wake him. Somehow I knew this wouldn't be an ordinary Sunday afternoon. It would be the last time I saw Hoover.

Lee Durbin - Hoover. Our hearts are broken. We watched as you thrived at Big Cat Rescue after being rescued from horrendous conditions in a circus in Peru. We watched as you were shown more love, care and compassion in three years than you received in the first 12 years of your life. And now you are gone.

I first watched the rescue video of Hoover in 2016 and it is what drew me to BCR. I saw this magnificent tiger be rescued from a cage, until he took his first steps into a beautiful enclosure with trees, grass and water, something he had never known. I cried. I must have watched that video a hundred times while sharing with friends to explain why big cats do not belong in cages. You were, and will always be, a beacon for big cats everywhere with your story, shining a light on the abuse of big cats being kept in cages and backyard zoos.

I loved to watch him playing in the water and with his boomer ball. He loved to tease his keepers and see how long of a stick they would have to use to feed him while he lounged in his den. I almost think it was a game to him, and one that the very dedicated keepers were willing to play with him to get him to eat. We all cheered online when he ate his food! Big Cat Rescue keepers, staff, and online followers will forever remember you. You were one of a kind to us and will always be in our hearts. We love and miss you Hoover.

Nancy Both - Camop Nan - Hoover was a symbol of hope. He overcame such great odds to survive the Peruvian Circus and make his way to Big Cat Rescue. Even after arriving at BCR he continued to face health challenges and overcame them with the great care he received from the marvelous staff and keepers there. Our sweet Hoover definitely challenged his keepers, but they never gave up on him. Watching them coax him to eat by using a long stick to feed him while he lounged in his den, were truly memorable moments. Thank you Hoover for being one of the most memorable tigers I've followed on the explore cams and BCR for giving us the opportunity to get to know him.

Mindy Berman-Bertone - The first time I visited BCR, Hoover was just chilling up against his enclosure. As I stood there he gave THE BIGGEST YAWN I had ever seen and I got a picture at that exact moment. It was awesome! I loved his personality, his sauntering, his teasing the keepers, "Yes I'll eat, eh, maybe not, oh what do you have, eh not today". Lol. Mr Stubborn Pants. He was a fun tiger to watch and I'm so glad he lived his last 3 years enjoying his life. He was magnificent to see when I came to visit. You are very missed our Governor of The Tampanghetti

Kristine Metzner Cam Op - I remember Carole talking about rescuing a Tiger from Peru and waiting for the paperwork and waiting.....and waiting.....

Then the time came for Hoover to fly to his forever home at Big Cat Rescue. I stayed up all night until 9am in the morning to watch the updates of his travel and then see him step foot into his wonderful new home. I watched with tears running down my face, as he saw and experienced water for the first time. He captured my heart that day and brought a renewed awareness of the plight of circus cats and animals.

I loved every minute of following him around with the Explore camera. He would always look directly at the camera, like he knew we were there watching him. I loved seeing his personality come out and watching his playful antics. He was the most beautiful and special Tiger ever. I know his life will not be in vain.......I know one day, wild animals in circuses will be banned worldwide forever. I can't wait for that day.... for Hoover and all wild cats that have to endure the abuse of circuses, cub petting schemes, etc..

Hoover will always be My Forever Tiger Love.....I forever love him and miss him..... Run free Hoover with your clan and all the Tigers that went before....run free in the fields of Heaven. Love you sweet, precious boy. <3

Rux Cam Op - I will never be able to express what I felt and feel for him, how much this tiger gave me, he changed my life. Hoover was magical. Hoover was a dream. My dream, everyone's dream. A dream which became real for him and everyone. A dream that inspired me to follow my dreams and never give up. I will always follow this dream with my magical boy. He will always be with me now and I with him.
Love you forever my magical boy.

Christine Saucier Cam Op - It always lifted me to see the keepers' patience and persistence pay off when, after many, many attempts, he finally ate!

Christine Saucier Cam Op - Thanks to BCR for the simple pleasures Hoover enjoyed in his final few years.

Christine Saucier Cam Op - "When you're lost in the nightmare of life, just hold my hand, and follow the sound of my heartbeat to find sanctuary in my heart."
― Anthony T. Hincks

7th-grade English teacher Stacy Reeves - "Dear Barbara and the BCR Family, My seventh-grade students wanted to make you guys a card to let you know how sorry they are about the loss of beautiful Hoover.

Two of my students designed the artwork on the front, and they put a message on the back. The artwork is their vision of Hoover looking down from Heaven above BCR. The bottom half is a map of Big Cat Rescue. They also wanted to add the dragonflies after I read them the touching announcement of Hoover's passing. They have thoroughly enjoyed the photos and videos of "their" tigers: Sapphire, Priya, and Dutchess. They have taken to calling them "our babies."

We have laughed and cried, but most of all, they are becoming aware of and talking about the plight of big cats. You have earned a young, captive audience. Thank you for all you do. All our best, Stacy

"Hoover"

Hoover arrived at Big Cat Rescue on Saturday, April 23rd, which was his birthday.

Hoover was a former circus tiger from Peru.

Hoover died of kidney failure and other age-related problems.

4/23/04 ✻ 10/17/19

Rest in Peace, "Hoover."

Keeper Bonnie Farago - Hoover's enclosure was right outside our enrichment barn, and it was such a joy to watch him while we made enrichment. He had such a quiet, graceful presence about him that made him seem so powerful. Even through everything be had been through.... circus performing, traveling to the USA, several surgeries.....he still kept his sweet and trusting demeanor. You will be missed sweet Hoover. We are so blessed that you got to spend your last years with us. Enjoy paradise.

Bonnie (Viewer/Online Volunteer) - One chilly morning I was scrolling through my newsfeed on Facebook and a post/video caught my eye, regarding a tiger rescue. The tiger's name was Hoover and he was being rescued from a circus in Peru. From that day on, I fell in love with a tiger named Hoover.

From viewing that post/video, I was fortunate enough to discover Big Cat Rescue. Hoover was special to me in so many ways. He not only touched by heart, he touched my soul. My daily routine would consist of viewing his webcam, reading posts, or watching videos where he was the featured cat. All was right in the world, as long as my Hoover was safe, loved, and cared for.

Hoover will remain in my heart forever and I miss him so much! Everywhere I go, Hoover is right there with me, reminding me to be strong, courageous, and never give up on myself no matter what odds come against me. RIP precious Hoover. You truly were a one of a kind tiger.

SUMMARY of Big Cat Rescue's HISTORY & EVOLUTION
By Carole Baskin, Founder of Big Cat Rescue

Animal abusers hate us because we are the leading sanctuary dedicated to ending the abuse at its root by banning the private possession of exotic cats. These big cat abusers make up lies or twist the truth to make people think that we breed, buy, sell, and allow public contact (just like they still do). We never bred lions or tigers. Our first kitten was born in 1994 and we stopped breeding in 1997.
There were a couple of accidents, from older cats and hybrids that we didn't think were fertile, but the very last cat born there was a leopard cat in 2001. His parents were both in their late teens and thought to be too old to breed. As of 2015, we have rescued more than 200 exotic cats. We now have a total of 3 that were born here.

Big Cat Rescue did not start out as what it has become today. My beliefs and the sanctuary that reflects them, evolved over time. It involved lessons that came from what I view today as horrible mistakes, and sometimes I feel terrible about how long some realizations took. But I take great pride in what we have become and are accomplishing and feel great excitement about what I believe we will accomplish in the future.

The sanctuary began when the search to purchase a pet bobcat kitten brought us unwittingly to a "fur farm" that sold a few cats as pets, but primarily raised them to turn into fur coats. We bought all 56 kittens to save them from being slaughtered.

To learn how to take care of the cats we naturally turned to those who would know, the breeders and owners of exotic cats. Under this influence, initially we believed what you will still hear from the breeders and owners today, i.e. that these cats should be owned privately to "preserve the species," that they make good pets if properly raised and trained, and that they are safe if you know how to handle them.
In addition to buying cats, we had started breeding some cats under the misguided notion that this was a way to "preserve the species." A few of our cats were purchased with this in mind, although invariably we were also giving them a home far better than what they were destined for if we did not purchase them. I had not then figured out what seems so obvious to me today, that breeding for life in a cage an animal that was meant to roam free was inherently cruel, and that most of the "homes" these animals would end up in were places where they would live in unsuitable conditions. We believe these cats should not be pets.

Since those early years the sanctuary has pursued its vision of ending the abuse and abandonment of captive exotic animals and promoting preservation of the species in the wild.
We do this by being an "educational sanctuary" with the dual <u>mission</u> of (a) giving our cats the best care we can while (b) educating the public on the plight of these animals so that someday there will be no need for a sanctuary to exist.

Increasingly the plight of these wonderful animals is resonating with the general public. As a result, recently our efforts and those of others like us, to encourage laws forbidding breeding and exotic pet ownership have met with escalating success.
State after state has passed laws banning ownership of big cats. They vary in effectiveness largely due to what "exemptions" from the law are allowed. But, the trend in state law and public opinion is clear. In 2012, working with a coalition of other animal protection organizations, a federal bill banning possession and breeding except in very limited circumstances was passed.

As we have become a leading and very visible voice not only in support of such legislation but being asked by legislators to help draft the bills, the breeders, exotic pet owners and exhibitors have attacked me. Lacking substantive arguments in support of their beliefs and activities, which I believe are based on selfish enjoyment of having the animals and/or financial gain, they have spent considerable energy attacking me personally and our sanctuary.

They claim we hide the activities from our early years that you have read about here, which obviously we do not and we never have. While I am not proud that it took me years of seeing increasing amounts of abuse to reverse the beliefs that I accepted as a novice, I believe the experience from those years has been heavily responsible for the success we have been having. I understand the thinking of the pet trade because I was part of it. I believe we are more credible as a source of objective information specifically because we came from the place in which our opponents remain entrenched.

I genuinely hope that over time their thinking will change the way mine has done. In the meantime, I would like to thank from the bottom of my heart all of the many wonderful volunteers and thousands of generous financial supporters and "Advocats" without whose hard work we would not be seeing the recent successes.

Read more about this at https://BigCatRescue.org

BIG CATS MAKE BAD PETS

Tampa is home to the world's largest sanctuary for abused, abandoned and retired exotic cats. Big Cat Rescue has housed many lions, tigers, cougars, leopards, bobcats, servals and others, 16 species in all. Most were former pets abandoned by their owners.

The narrow mission of Big Cat Rescue is to provide a good home for the limited number of cats that the sanctuary can afford to take in. But we can only save a small percentage of those in need. The sanctuary must turn away over 100 cats each year. Because of this, the broader mission of the sanctuary is to reduce the number of cats that suffer the fate of abandonment and abuse by educating as many people as possible about the conditions that lead to the plight of these animals and how they can help.

There are two major sources of the abuse and abandonment. The first is the "pet trade", the breeders who sell these wild animals to people as pets and the people who buy them. The second largest source of the animals is the "entertainment" or "edu-tainment" industry, a subject for another day.

Most of our cats come to us because people buy them as pets and then cannot handle them. Breeders lie and tell people that if the cat is fixed it will not spray so they can keep them inside. Not true. The spray is so acidic it eats through our galvanized cage wire over time. When they spray drywall, you do not clean it – you replace it.

Even kept outside, the cats usually make terrible pets. They are adorable cubs when purchased. Having these "cool" unusual pets, the owners get the attention from other people that humans tend to crave. But the cats live for 20 years if well cared for, and as they mature, they become increasingly problematic as instinct takes over. Their "play" is rough because their skin is thick enough to withstand it. Ours is not, so even their affection can be deadly. It is pure instinct for them to attack children, other pets, or anyone whose back is turned.

They do not typically seek or give affection the way we are used to from domestic animals. There is no kennel to take them when you travel, and whom do you ask to come feed your 150-pound carnivorous cougar? Many are abandoned because the owner's personal circumstances change. We get them because people get married, get divorced, get sick, die, get bitten, or just get tired of the heavy burden of caring for them.

In addition to the bad experience pet owners have, most of the wild cats purchased as pets have a horrible existence. A large percentage die as tiny kittens because owners do not know how to bottle feed them. Of those that live, huge numbers suffer malnutrition due to owner ignorance of their nutritional needs. And most live a horrible life in cages that, while often legal, do not meet their physical or psychological needs.

There are countless reasons that non-domestic cats should not be pets, and no reasons other than human ego for allowing them to be pets. Individuals can help end this constant stream of abused, abandoned and destroyed animals by not purchasing them as pets and by supporting laws, regulations, and the enforcement of those laws and regulations to end pet ownership of exotic cats.

BIG CAT RESCUE'S MISSION STATEMENT

Our Mission is to provide the best home we can for the cats in our care, end abuse of big cats in captivity, and prevent extinction of big cats in the wild.

You can join us in the freedom fight for exotic cats! They were designed to live free; not in cages. The number one cause of abuse is the practice of posing with big cats and their cubs because it creates a flood of discarded cats that serve no conservation value and end up dead or in conditions that are often even worse.

MAKE THE CALL OF THE WILD
Tell Congress to end big cat abuse!

An estimated 10,000 to 20,000 big cats languish in deplorable conditions in backyards, roadside zoos, and traveling exhibits throughout the US. Tigers, lions, and other big cats should not be kept as pets or used for abusive cub petting schemes. While some states have regulations that attempt to protect big cats, decades of experience have proven they don't work.

The only solution is to pass the Big Cat Public Safety Act (HR 1380) - federal legislation that would end owning big cats as pets and stop cub petting, the #1 cause of big cat abuse. You can make sure this law gets passed by contacting your members of Congress and asking them to end ownership of big cats as pets and abusive cub petting by co-sponsoring the Big Cat Public Safety Act when it is reintroduced in Congress!

Take action by visiting **BigCatAct.com** or by texting the word CATS to 52886 and using the tools there to make the Call of the Wild.

Honor Hoover, by making the Call of the Wild, every week until the Big Cat Pubic Safety Act becomes law.

Hoover's Curly Tail Photos by Brittany Mira
Hoover's adorable curly tail always made us smile.

Visit us at:

https://BigCatRescue.org
http://Facebook.com/bigcatrescue
http://BigCatCams.com
http://ARZoo.me

Acknowledgements

Text by Holly Kopacz

I would like to thank the TRULY AMAZING photographers for their generous contributions for Hoover's Memorial Book. Profits from this book have been donated to Big Cat Rescue to help care for cats like Hoover. Without their photos this book would not be possible.

Most of the photos were taken by Brittany Mira, Jamie Veronica, & Mary Lou Geis. The remaining photos are by various Keepers, Interns, Partners, Guests, & Staff. Not all donated for BCR use had names on them. As I find out who those are I will edit future editions of this book.

Back Cover Art by Jessica Marks
Front Cover Art by Debbie Perrott

Layout & Distribution LaWanna Mitchell

Shop to Save Big Cat at:

http://BigCatRescue.biz
http://BigCatRescue.org/amazonstore
http://CatRescue.biz
https://teespring.com/stores/bigcatrescue

Made in the USA
Middletown, DE
03 January 2020